Just BecAuse I am...
Doesn't Mean...

Stan Pearson II

D1532320

First Edition: 2009

Cover Designs and Layout by Abra Johnson, AbraJohnson@Mac.com
Editing by Kristin Walinski, www.ScribeOnDemand.com

Just Because I am... Doesn't Mean... / Stan Pearson II

Further information on this book
and the work of
Stan Pearson II
available at:

www.StanPearson.com

ISBN 978-1-442-17032-2

This book is dedicated to all people who want to learn more about themselves and the people whose lives intersect with them now or will intersect with them in the future.

These feelings, thoughts, and expressions will help enlighten us all as we move forward in our diverse worlds...

PREFACE

This collection of thoughts is more powerful than the words on the page. These thoughts lurk in our minds and hearts. We don't often share them or put them into the atmosphere for fear of what others may think.

Now is the time to speak and let our thoughts, voices, and emotions be heard as we move toward better days and more understanding times.

FOREWORD

*Just because I am a friend, a colleague, a
practitioner doesn't mean . . .*

When I first saw this program, it made me realize the
number of categories in which I could put myself or be labeled
as. Then, all at once, many emotions rushed over me. I got a
little frustrated, mad, and confused, which led me to pick a
final "just because":

*Just because I am a category doesn't
mean I am not an individual!*

This thought made me smile. I realized being an
individual means it is okay to break out of your box, shatter a
paradigm, or bend the rules that are generally recognized.

Stan Pearson's presentation and book are meant to make
you think. They intend to make you laugh. They intend to
start a dialogue. They intend to open your eyes. They intend
to cause change.

When you read through the statements in Just Because people have been brave enough to share, allow the words to open your thoughts. I say "brave" because it takes a lot to share that you are something but that doesn't mean you are not something else. Some readers and participants will comment because they think what they read and hear is funny, but what makes the statements funny is that each contains a grain of truth.

The truth in this book and Stan's ability to bring the truth to light is refreshing. As someone who continues to learn, it is empowering for me to see, hear, and participate in a time when we recognize that each reader or participant's thoughts can break biases and prejudices.

What unites us are our commonalities (the "just because"), but what makes us learn and grow and what makes the world a better place (the "doesn't mean") is our individuality. I challenge you, after you read this book, to ask your family, friends, and colleagues to create their own statements of recognition and change.

- Dennis Koch, Director of Residence Life, Texas A&M University–Commerce

Religions are many and diverse, but reason and goodness are one.

- Elbert Hubbard
American writer, publisher, and artist

- Just because I am white doesn't mean I am privileged.

- Just because I am a single mother doesn't mean I can't make it alone.

Your Reflections:

- Just because I am Mexican doesn't mean I am Catholic.

- Just because I am homosexual doesn't mean I am promiscuous.

Your Reflections:

- Just because I am mixed doesn't mean I can't identify with multiple cultures.

- Just because I am black doesn't mean I live in the ghetto.

Your Reflections:

- Just because I wear glasses doesn't mean I am a nerd.

- Just because I am in band doesn't mean I am a dork.

Your Reflections:

- Just because I am overweight doesn't mean I like to eat.

- Just because I am a woman doesn't mean I can't be the boss.

Your Reflections:

- Just because I am of Latino decent doesn't mean I speak Spanish.

- Just because I was born into poverty doesn't mean I will remain in poverty.

Your Reflections:

- Just because I am white doesn't mean I only listen to country music.

- Just because I am black doesn't mean I can't speak a second language.

Your Reflections:

- Just because I am Christian doesn't mean I will push my beliefs on you.

- Just because I am Mexican doesn't mean I crossed the border illegally.

Your Reflections:

- Just because I am black doesn't mean I have nappy hair.

- Just because I am a nontraditional student doesn't mean I am not intelligent.

Your Reflections:

One day our descendants will think it incredible that we paid so much attention to things like the amount of melanin in our skin or the shape of our eyes or our gender instead of the unique identities of each of us as complex human beings.

– Franklin Thomas, The Liberty of the Citizen

- Just because I am ditzy doesn't mean I am dumb.

- Just because I like to party doesn't mean I drink.

Your Reflections:

_____
_____
_____
_____
_____
_____
_____
_____
_____
_____
_____
_____
_____
_____
_____
_____
_____
_____
_____
_____
_____
_____
_____
_____

- Just because I am Hispanic doesn't mean I am lazy.

- Just because I am skinny doesn't mean I am not strong.

Your Reflections:

- Just because I am white doesn't mean I am racist.

- Just because I dress well doesn't mean I am gay.

Your Reflections:

- Just because I am a man doesn't mean I can't be sensitive.

- Just because I am a man doesn't mean I can't cook.

Your Reflections:

- Just because I am a woman doesn't mean I can't make more money than a man.

- Just because I am from the Middle East doesn't mean I am a terrorist.

Your Reflections:

- Just because I am from Colombia doesn't mean I sell drugs.

- Just because I am white doesn't mean I am not discriminated against.

Your Reflections:

- Just because I was raised in a single-parent home doesn't mean I won't be successful.

- Just because I am a teacher doesn't mean I will only marry a lawyer.

Your Reflections:

- Just because I am tall doesn't mean I am an athlete.

- Just because I am a female athlete doesn't mean I am a lesbian.

Your Reflections:

- Just because I speak proper English doesn't mean I am a sellout.

- Just because I am an athlete doesn't mean I don't like modern dance or ballet.

Your Reflections:

The price of the democratic way of life is a growing appreciation of people's differences, not merely as tolerable, but as the essence of a rich and rewarding human experience.

– Jerome Nathanson, journalist

- Just because I am African-American doesn't mean I can dance.

- Just because I am Caucasian doesn't mean I can't dance.

Your Reflections:

- Just because I am Asian doesn't mean I only like math.

- Just because I am African doesn't mean I am Muslim.

Your Reflections:

- Just because I am a Democrat doesn't mean I don't have conservative views.

- Just because I am a successful athlete doesn't mean I take performance-enhancing drugs.

Your Reflections:

- Just because I dress in black/gothic clothes doesn't mean I am not like everyone else.

- Just because I am a woman doesn't mean I am not strong.

Your Reflections:

- Just because I am a cop doesn't mean I eat doughnuts all day.

- Just because I wear braids doesn't mean I am a thug.

Your Reflections:

- Just because I am Jewish doesn't mean I am affluent or frugal.

- Just because I am kind doesn't mean I am weak.

Your Reflections:

- Just because I am a blonde doesn't mean I don't have brains.

- Just because I am black doesn't mean I think it's okay to use the "N" word.

Your Reflections:

- Just because I am young doesn't mean I am immature.

- Just because I am Hispanic doesn't mean I came from a big family.

Your Reflections:

- Just because I am not wealthy doesn't mean I steal.

- Just because I am black doesn't mean I only eat soul food.

Your Reflections:

The wave of the future is not the conquest of the world by a single dogmatic creed but the liberation of the diverse energies of free nations and free men.

– John F. Kennedy, President of the United States

- Just because I am Mexican doesn't mean I like beans.

- Just because I am Asian doesn't mean I only eat fried rice.

Your Reflections:

- Just because I am Asian doesn't mean all Asians look alike.

- Just because I am black doesn't mean I rap.

Your Reflections:

- Just because I am heavyset doesn't mean I am not beautiful.

- Just because I don't go to church doesn't mean I don't believe in God.

Your Reflections:

- Just because I live on a farm doesn't mean I am uneducated.

- Just because I said "hi" doesn't mean I like you.

Your Reflections:

- Just because I accepted the drink/dinner you bought me doesn't mean I am your girlfriend.

- Just because I chat online doesn't mean I am weird.

Your Reflections:

- Just because I look white doesn't mean I am white.

- Just because I am Asian doesn't mean I am Chinese.

Your Reflections:

- Just because I am dressed in sweats doesn't mean I am poor.

- Just because I am Hispanic/Latin American doesn't mean I am Mexican.

Your Reflections:

- Just because I drive an old car doesn't mean I am not successful.

- Just because I like to have fun doesn't mean I am irresponsible.

Your Reflections:

- Just because I am a blue collar worker doesn't mean I am stupid.

- Just because I am a cheerleader doesn't mean I am a snob.

Your Reflections:

Since when do you have to agree with people
to defend them from injustice?

– Lillian Hellman, American playwright

- Just because I am an only child doesn't mean I am spoiled.

- Just because I am agnostic doesn't mean I don't have morals.

Your Reflections:

- Just because I am Irish doesn't mean I am a drunk.

- Just because I am German doesn't mean my family is racist.

Your Reflections:

- Just because I am a female doesn't mean I am clueless when it comes to sports.

- Just because I am Hispanic doesn't mean I can't play a leading role in a movie.

Your Reflections:

- Just because I wait tables doesn't mean I am uneducated.

- Just because I am from a small town doesn't mean I am naïve.

Your Reflections:

- Just because I am male doesn't mean I won't ask for directions.

- Just because I am female doesn't mean I can't drive.

Your Reflections:

- Just because I am deaf doesn't mean I can't dance.

- Just because I am disabled doesn't mean I am not capable of success.

Your Reflections:

- Just because I am rich doesn't mean I am happy.

- Just because I live in the ghetto doesn't mean I am "ghetto."

Your Reflections:

- Just because I am white doesn't mean my mother isn't black.

- Just because my name is Tyrone doesn't mean I am black.

Your Reflections:

- Just because I am a successful black man doesn't mean I will marry a white woman.

- Just because I am a minority doesn't mean I am a womanizer.

Your Reflections:

When Jesus Christ asked little children to come to him, he didn't say only rich children, or White children, or children with two-parent families, or children who didn't have a mental or physical handicap. He said, "Let all children come unto me."

– Marian Wright Edelman, American activist
for children's rights

- Just because I have a tattoo doesn't mean I am easy.

- Just because I look young doesn't mean I am not a groomed professional.

Your Reflections:

- Just because you have a diverse circle of acquaintances doesn't mean you're not racist.

- Just because I am a black man who dates outside of my race doesn't mean I don't love black women.

Your Reflections:

- Just because I am Mexican doesn't mean I am corrupt.

- Just because I am white doesn't mean I can't play basketball.

Your Reflections:

- Just because I am Mexican doesn't mean I like Tejano music.

- Just because I am small doesn't mean I am simple.

Your Reflections:

- Just because I am not poor doesn't mean I don't need financial aid.

- Just because I am Mexican doesn't mean I like Mexican food.

Your Reflections:

- Just because I am a cheerleader doesn't mean I am an airhead.

- Just because I am a woman doesn't mean I have to do the dishes.

Your Reflections:

- Just because I am a woman doesn't mean I can't protect myself.

- Just because I am Asian doesn't mean school comes easy.

Your Reflections:

- Just because I am Asian doesn't mean I have an accent.

- Just because I am smart doesn't mean I love Harry Potter.

Your Reflections:

_____

_____

_____

_____

_____

_____

_____

_____

_____

_____

_____

_____

_____

_____

_____

_____

_____

_____

_____

_____

- Just because I am Asian doesn't mean my eyes are shaped funny.

- Just because I am Jamaican doesn't mean I smoke marijuana.

Your Reflections:

Parents can only give good advice or put them on the right paths, but the final forming of a person's character lies in their own hands.

– Anne Frank, Novelist, persecuted in the holocaust

- Just because I am French doesn't mean I don't take showers.

- Just because I am poor doesn't mean I am invisible.

Your Reflections:

- Just because I am German doesn't mean I am a Nazi.

- Just because I am in a fraternity or sorority doesn't mean I drink and have wild parties.

Your Reflections:

- Just because I am in a fraternity or sorority doesn't mean I buy my friends.

- Just because I am gay doesn't mean I don't have morals.

Your Reflections:

- Just because I am from Texas doesn't mean I am a cowboy.

- Just because I am a guy doesn't mean I cheat in relationships.

Your Reflections:

- Just because I have tattoos doesn't mean I am in a gang.

- Just because I am from the barrio doesn't mean I won't be successful.

Your Reflections:

- Just because I am a minority doesn't mean I won't run this country some day.

- Just because I am from the South doesn't mean I am a redneck.

Your Reflections:

- Just because I am Mexican doesn't mean I don't have a firm grasp on the English language.

- Just because I was born in Mexico doesn't mean I am a wetback.

Your Reflections:

- Just because I am Italian doesn't mean my family is in the mob.

- Just because I want a successful companion doesn't mean I am a gold digger.

Your Reflections:

- Just because I am a minority doesn't mean I should use racial slurs.

- Just because I wear all black doesn't mean I am weird or dangerous.

Your Reflections:

People grow through experience if they meet life honestly and courageously. This is how character is built.

– Eleanor Roosevelt, First Lady

- Just because I smile at you doesn't mean I want you.

- Just because I am homeless doesn't mean I'll always be.

Your Reflections:

- Just because I am adopted doesn't mean I am abandoned.

- Just because I am part of a group doesn't mean I am not my own person.

Your Reflections:

_____

_____

_____

_____

_____

_____

_____

_____

_____

_____

_____

_____

_____

_____

_____

_____

_____

_____

_____

_____

- Just because you see me doesn't mean I don't feel invisible.

- Just because I flirt doesn't mean I am unfaithful.

Your Reflections:

- Just because I look black doesn't mean I am black.

- Just because I am one religion doesn't mean I don't agree with parts of others.

Your Reflections:

- Just because we argued doesn't mean I stopped thinking of you.

- Just because I give you advice doesn't mean I am controlling.

Your Reflections:

- Just because I am scared doesn't mean I won't overcome my fear.

- Just because I am not financially stable right now doesn't mean I won't be.

Your Reflections:

- Just because sports seem to be my life doesn't mean I don't have other interests.

- Just because I look menacing doesn't mean I am.

Your Reflections:

- Just because I crossed the border illegally doesn't mean I am not a worthy human being.

- Just because I have rims on my car doesn't mean I am a drug dealer.

Your Reflections:

- Just because I am a different minority doesn't mean we're not in this together.

- Just because we are divided by others doesn't mean we cannot unite each other.

Your Reflections:

Change will not come if we wait for some other person or some other time. We are the ones we've been waiting for. We are the change that we seek.

– Barack Obama, President of the United States

If you don't stand for something, you'll fall for anything.

– Malcolm X, American Black Nationalist leader

I look forward confidently to the day when all who work for a living will be one with no thought to their separateness as Negroes, Jews, Italians or any other distinctions. This will be the day when we bring into full realization the American dream—a dream yet unfulfilled. A dream of equality of opportunity, of privilege and property widely distributed; a dream of a land where men will not take necessities from the many to give luxuries to the few; a dream of a land where men will not argue that the color of a man's skin determines the content of his character; a dream of a nation where all our gifts and resources are held not for ourselves alone, but as instruments of service for the rest of humanity; the dream of a country where every man will respect the dignity and worth of the human personality.

– Martin Luther King, Jr., Civil Rights Leader

Afterword

Every time I travel or present at institutions, businesses, or special events, I find myself observing and marveling at all of the possibilities. We often pass up many opportunities to grow because of our past experiences.

Most days we go to sleep with at least one question in our head we could have asked someone. Were we afraid of the response? Were we afraid of our accountability once we know the answer? Knowing is a real commitment. Once we are made aware of or are educated about an issue or experience, we are no longer ignorant. We can no longer play the "I didn't know better" game.

We stand to gain so much more if we own each and every experience we have, both good and bad. It would be magical if we only had great experiences and theme music played with every step we took; however, that is not realistic. Our great moments are much more enjoyable because we experienced turmoil or obstacles before achieving them.

We cannot help but to be prejudiced. However controversial that sounds, it is very close to the truth. Our first encounters are typically initiated by sight, touch, or smell. What is most important about these first encounters is how we react to them and how we continue to act afterward. I challenge you to open up. When you have an open vessel, more can flow through it. When you have these encounters, you can openly think to yourself that person is different, that experience is different, or that situation is different, but that difference will not stop me from growing and learning.

Every statement you read in this book represented a feeling. Each statement is meant to be thought-provoking. It is meant to start a conversation that will live and breathe. As a result, before you seek change in anyone or anything else, you should seek change in yourself.

When was the last time you woke up and said, "Yes, today is going to be a great day?" You didn't say that because the sun was shining or because you knew your car was going to start, but because you knew you could handle whatever experience or person the day threw at you. That is Diversity, that is Leadership, and that is Success. Ultimately, it is what we are made of.

Dr. Wayne Dyer, who is considered the "Father of Motivation" by his fans, suggests we be in a constant state of awe: so many experiences to recognize and enjoy surround us, including nature, relationships, and even just waking up every morning. Take time to appreciate your surroundings and circumstances, whether you are driving, traveling, or meeting someone. Dr. Dyer also teaches that sometimes our egos don't allow us to open up to other experiences or individuals—they do not allow us to accept ourselves or anyone else.

Have you ever just wanted to be accepted or to be seen as equal in any way, whether it be racially, educationally, socioeconomically, spiritually, or some other way? We have to sort through "just because

I am . . ." just as everyone else does. When you look at a "just because," think about it, and grow from your thoughts, it is a powerful and transformational experience. I challenge you to always define yourself before anything or anyone else.

You are strong, and yes, you are different. Being different is beautiful, and it is more than okay. Hold on to who you are, because you are part of what makes living so great. Being different is dynamic.

When you wake up in the morning and look in the mirror, tell yourself, "I am beautiful because I am different and when God made me, he was showing off." Once you make a habit out of thinking these positive thoughts, you become a product of those thoughts.

Thank you for reading, participating, growing, and being who you are every day. Diversity is everything we experience, and we succeed because of it.

Just because we have finished reading, doesn't mean our journey is done...

DIVERSITY
DIARY

97